WORLD SOCCER CLUBS

LIVERPOOL

by David J. Clarke

Copyright © 2025 by Press Room Editions. All rights reserved. No part of this book may be used or reproduced in any manner whatsoever, including internet usage, without written permission from the copyright owner, except in the case of brief quotations embodied in critical articles and reviews.

Book design by Kate Liestman
Cover design by Kate Liestman

Photographs ©: Andrew Yates/Sportimage/Cal Sport Media/AP Images, cover; Clive Brunskill/Getty Images Sport/Getty Images, 5, 7, 8; EMPPL PA Wire/AP Images, 11; Allsport UK/Allsport/Getty Images Sport/Getty Images, 12; Peter Byrne/EMPPL PA Wire/AP Images, 15; Gary M. Prior/Allsport/Getty Images Sport/Getty Images, 17; Peter Kemp/AP Images, 19; Liewig Christian/Corbis Sport/Getty Images, 21; Alex Grimm/Bongarts/Getty Images, 23; Richard Heathcote/Getty Images Sport/Getty Images, 25; Laurence Griffiths/Getty Images Sport/Getty Images, 27; Julian Finney/Getty Images Sport/Getty Images, 29

Press Box Books, an imprint of Press Room Editions.

ISBN
978-1-63494-959-0 (library bound)
978-1-63494-973-6 (paperback)
979-8-89469-004-9 (epub)
978-1-63494-987-3 (hosted ebook)

Library of Congress Control Number: 2024940876

Distributed by North Star Editions, Inc.
2297 Waters Drive
Mendota Heights, MN 55120
www.northstareditions.com

Printed in the United States of America
012025

ABOUT THE AUTHOR

David J. Clarke is a freelance sportswriter. Originally from Helena, Montana, he now lives in Savannah, Georgia.

TABLE OF CONTENTS

CHAPTER 1
A COMEBACK AT ANFIELD 4

CHAPTER 2
BUILDING LIVERPOOL 10

CHAPTER 3
TRAGEDIES AND TRIUMPHS . . . 16

CHAPTER 4
PRESSING FOR GLORY 22

SUPERSTAR PROFILE
MOHAMED SALAH 28

QUICK STATS 30
GLOSSARY 31
TO LEARN MORE 32
INDEX 32

CHAPTER 1

A COMEBACK AT ANFIELD

On May 7, 2019, Liverpool needed a miracle. Six days earlier, Liverpool had lost to Barcelona 3–0 in the first leg of their Champions League semifinal. But the round wasn't over. The teams still had to play at Anfield, Liverpool's home stadium. The team with the most goals after both games would win. Liverpool fans hoped for a comeback.

Liverpool fans display a banner of their European titles before facing Barcelona in the 2019 Champions League semifinal.

Liverpool came out flying. Striker Divock Origi scored in the first half. Midfielder Georginio Wijnaldum then added two more goals early in the second half. The next goal would likely send one team to the final.

Liverpool earned a corner kick in the 79th minute. Right back Trent Alexander-Arnold jogged over to place the ball. Winger Xherdan Shaqiri came over to take the kick. Liverpool's players moved into position in the penalty area. Normally, teams run routines on corner kicks. Everyone has to get into the right place before the ball is kicked.

Alexander-Arnold set the ball down and started to walk away. But he saw

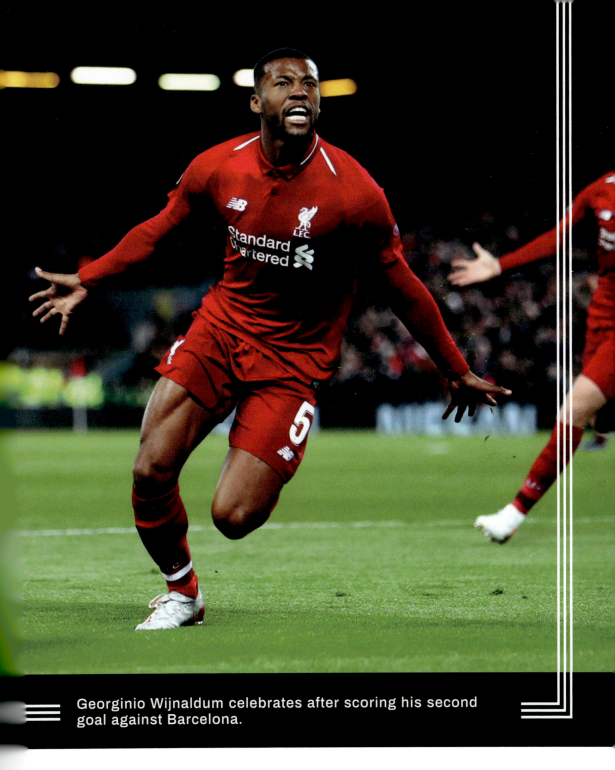

Georginio Wijnaldum celebrates after scoring his second goal against Barcelona.

Divock Origi (right) celebrates with his teammates after scoring the game-winning goal against Barcelona.

the Barcelona defenders weren't paying attention. Origi realized that, too. So, Alexander-Arnold quickly ran back to the corner. Then he crossed the ball into the penalty area. Origi tapped it into the goal. The Barcelona players looked stunned. Liverpool now led the game 4–0. More importantly, Liverpool had a 4–3 edge in total goals.

Liverpool held on to its lead. The Reds advanced to the Champions League final. Then they won that game 2–0 to claim the European title. It wouldn't have happened without an amazing comeback and some quick thinking.

ANOTHER GREAT ESCAPE

Liverpool barely made it out of the group stage of the 2018–19 Champions League. The Reds played Italian team Napoli on the final day of the group stage. If the Reds didn't win, they were out of the competition. Winger Mohamed Salah scored the game's only goal. Goalkeeper Alisson also made several key saves. Those stars helped Liverpool advance to the knockout round.

CHAPTER 2

BUILDING LIVERPOOL

Businessman John Houlding founded Liverpool Football Club in 1892. The club struggled early on. By 1947, Liverpool had won England's top league only five times. Then in 1954, Liverpool was relegated to the country's second division.

New manager Bill Shankly took over in 1959. Shankly was an energetic man

Ian Callaghan won five English league titles with Liverpool.

from Scotland. He encouraged the fans to be very loud at home games. Noise from the crowd could intimidate opponents. Shankly also changed the team's home uniforms from red and white to all red.

Shankly's changes worked. Liverpool played in front of roaring crowds. And the team started winning. Liverpool made it back to the top division in 1962. In 1963–64, the Reds won the title for the first time in 17 years. Star midfielder Ian Callaghan and high-scoring forward Roger Hunt led the way.

"YOU'LL NEVER WALK ALONE"

In 1945, the hit musical *Carousel* featured a song called "You'll Never Walk Alone." A new version of the song became popular in 1963. At the time, Liverpool played hit songs before games at Anfield. The crowd began singing along to "You'll Never Walk Alone." It quickly became a tradition. Liverpool fans still sing it before every home match.

Shankly won two more league titles with Liverpool. Then he retired in 1974. Assistant Bob Paisley took over. In nine seasons as manager, Paisley led the club to six league titles.

Liverpool played in the European Cup final in 1977. Tommy Smith scored a key goal in the 65th minute. Liverpool won the match 3–1 to claim its first European title. That tournament is now known as the Champions League. The best teams from Europe play in the competition each season. The Reds won the European Cup three more times in the next seven years.

Many legends played for Liverpool during this era. Kevin Keegan scored goals in bunches in the 1970s. He left

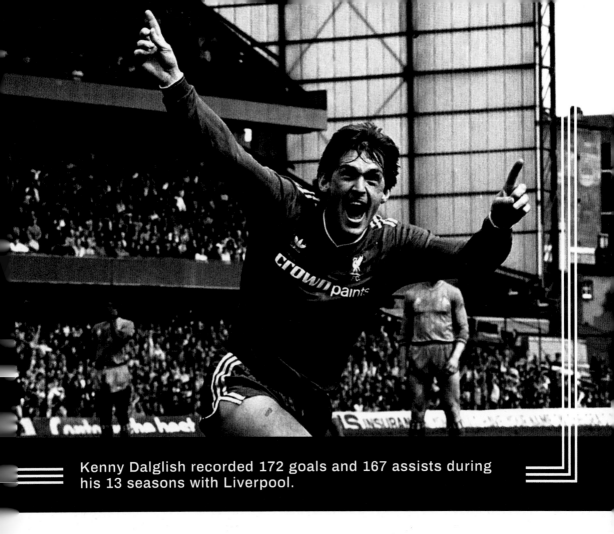

Kenny Dalglish recorded 172 goals and 167 assists during his 13 seasons with Liverpool.

in 1977. After that, Scotsman Kenny Dalglish became the team's star. Meanwhile, goalkeeper Ray Clemence kept the ball out of the net. Few teams could match Liverpool during this period. The good times wouldn't last, though.

CHAPTER 3

TRAGEDIES AND TRIUMPHS

On May 29, 1985, Liverpool was playing Italian team Juventus. Only a thin wall separated the two fan bases. Liverpool fans broke through it. While trying to escape, 39 people were crushed to death. Liverpool fans received blame for the tragedy. All English teams were banned from European games for five years.

Ian Rush played for Liverpool for 15 seasons. He scored a career-high 32 league goals during the 1983–84 season.

Liverpool remained successful in the English league. Strikers Ian Rush and John Aldridge led the club's attack. The Reds finished either first or second in the league every season from 1981–82 to 1990–91. However, another tragedy struck in 1989. The club was playing in the FA Cup. That tournament is England's top cup competition. Hillsborough Stadium in Sheffield, England, hosted the semifinal. A metal fence kept fans off the field. Too many Liverpool fans packed into the team's section. They pinned several fans against the fence. With nowhere to escape, 97 people were crushed to death.

Liverpool began to struggle in the 1990s. But in 2001–02, the Reds finally

Two days after the Hillsborough disaster, Liverpool fans gathered at Anfield to pay their respects to the victims of the tragedy.

finished high enough to reach the Champions League. New stars such as striker Michael Owen and midfielder Steven Gerrard led the way.

Liverpool reached the Champions League final in 2005. Playing in Istanbul,

Turkey, Liverpool quickly fell behind Italian team AC Milan. The Reds trailed 3–0 at halftime. Then Liverpool battled back. Gerrard scored in the 54th minute. Liverpool then added two more goals in the next six minutes. The game went to a penalty shootout. Liverpool goalkeeper Jerzy Dudek stopped two Milan penalties

THE MERSEYSIDE DERBY

Liverpool's closest rival is Everton. The two clubs both play in the city of Liverpool. Anfield is less than 1 mile (1.6 km) away from Goodison Park, Everton's home stadium. Matches between the two are called Merseyside derbies. They are named for the River Mersey, which runs through the city. The rivalry peaked in the 1980s. Liverpool won five English titles from 1981–82 to 1987–88. Everton won the other two.

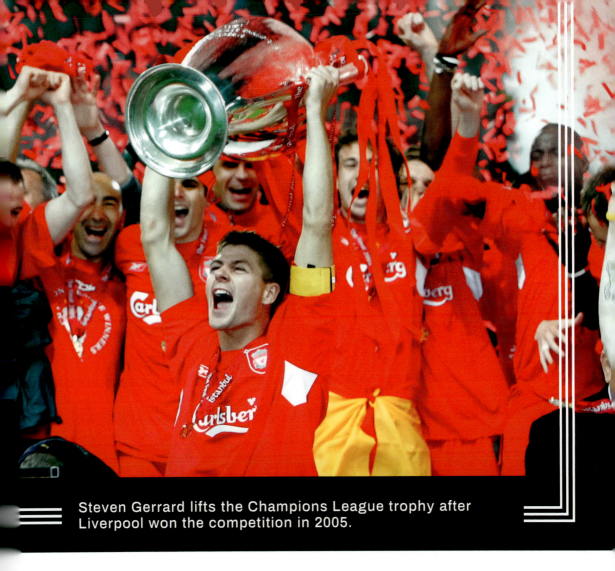

Steven Gerrard lifts the Champions League trophy after Liverpool won the competition in 2005.

in the shootout. His heroics helped the Reds win another European title. The victory became known as the "Miracle of Istanbul." It continued Liverpool's proud history of never giving up.

CHAPTER 4

PRESSING FOR GLORY

By 2015, Liverpool hadn't won an English league title since 1990. The Reds decided they needed a new manager. The team hired Jürgen Klopp. Klopp had won a lot in Germany. He coached his teams to play intense soccer. Under Klopp, Liverpool pressed its opponents all over the field. The

Jürgen Klopp was known for his fiery emotion on the sidelines during matches.

strategy created turnovers and easy scoring chances.

Liverpool quickly became one of England's most exciting teams. The Reds had several stars. Goalkeeper Alisson was one of world's best at his position. So were defenders Virgil van Dijk and Trent Alexander-Arnold. Liverpool's biggest strength was its forwards. Roberto Firmino, Sadio Mané, and Mohamed Salah piled up goals. This trio turned Liverpool into a powerhouse. In 2019, they lifted the Reds to the Champions League title.

In the English league, Liverpool finished second in 2018–19. The Reds lost only one game all season. Most years, Liverpool's 97 points would

Alisson makes a diving save during the 2019 Champions League final.

have been good enough to win the title. But rival Manchester City finished with 98. That set up a thrilling match in the 2019–20 season.

25

In November, the two teams met at Anfield. At the time, Liverpool was in first place by six points. Manchester City sat in second. Liverpool midfielder Fabinho started the game with a bang. He scored a thunderous goal from distance in the sixth minute. Salah then made it 2–0 with a header. Early in the second half, Mané put in another header. Liverpool won 3–1. The

A GAME OF CENTIMETERS

Manchester City delivered Liverpool's only loss of the 2018–19 season. And the Reds barely lost. In the 18th minute, a Liverpool rebound was just 1 centimeter (0.4 in) from crossing the goal line. But City defender John Stones cleared the ball before it fully crossed over. City went on to win 2–1.

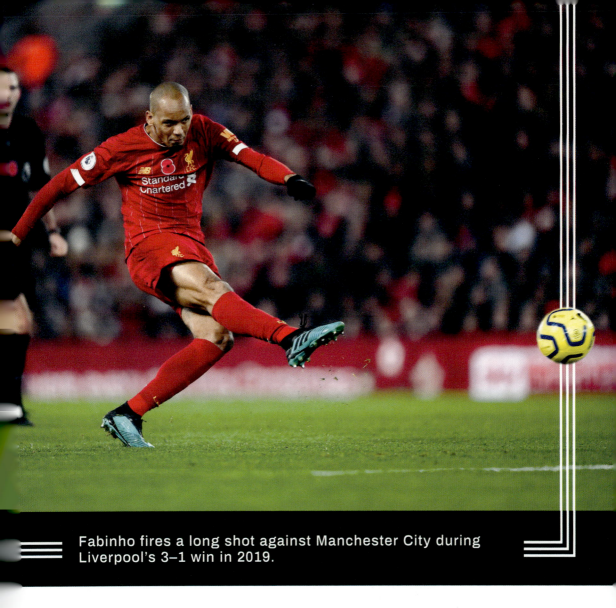

Fabinho fires a long shot against Manchester City during Liverpool's 3–1 win in 2019.

victory put the Reds up by eight points in the standings. No one came close to catching them. Liverpool was finally champion of England again.

SUPERSTAR PROFILE

MOHAMED SALAH

Mohamed Salah joined Liverpool in 2017. The speedy Egyptian thrived right away. Salah scored 50 goals in his first 65 games for Liverpool. No one in the club's long history had scored so many so fast.

Salah had incredibly quick feet. He used them to cut inside from the right wing. From there, he could blast shots with his lethal left foot. Salah also used his elite speed to burn defenders on counterattacks. When he didn't attempt to score, Salah often found an open teammate. His brilliant attacking play helped Liverpool become one of the best teams in Europe.

The winger seemed to do everything in a hurry. In a 2022 Champions League match, he came on as a substitute with 22 minutes left. It took him a little more than six minutes to score a hat trick. No player had ever scored a faster hat trick in Champions League history.

In Mohamed Salah's first season with Liverpool, he scored 44 goals in 52 games.

QUICK STATS

LIVERPOOL

Founded: 1892

Home stadium: Anfield

English league titles: 19

European Cup/Champions League titles: 6

FA Cup titles: 8

Key managers:

- Bill Shankly (1959–74): 3 English league titles, 2 FA Cup titles

- Bob Paisley (1974–83): 6 English league titles, 3 European Cup titles

- Jürgen Klopp (2015–24): 1 Premier League title, 1 Champions League title, 1 FA Cup title

Most career appearances: Ian Callaghan (857)

Most career goals: Ian Rush (336)

Stats are accurate through the 2023–24 season.

GLOSSARY

banned
Not allowed to take part in something.

hat trick
When a player scores three or more goals in a game.

knockout
A competition where one loss eliminates a team.

penalty area
The 18-yard box in front of the goal where a player is granted a penalty kick if he or she is fouled.

relegated
Sent down to a lower league because of a bad record.

rival
An opposing player or team that brings out the greatest emotion from fans and players.

shootout
A way of deciding a tie game. Players from each team take a series of penalty kicks.

TO LEARN MORE

Bougie, Matt. *Liverpool FC*. New York: Cavendish Square, 2021.

Hanlon, Luke. *The Best Matches of World Soccer*. Minneapolis: Abdo Publishing, 2024.

McDougall, Chrös. *The Best Rivalries of World Soccer*. Minneapolis: Abdo Publishing, 2024.

MORE INFORMATION

To learn more about Liverpool FC, go to **pressboxbooks.com/AllAccess**. These links are routinely monitored and updated to provide the most current information available.

INDEX

Aldridge, John, 18
Alexander-Arnold, Trent, 6, 8, 24
Alisson, 9, 24

Callaghan, Ian, 13
Clemence, Ray, 15

Dalglish, Kenny, 15
Dudek, Jerzy, 20

Fabinho, 26
Firmino, Roberto, 24

Gerrard, Steven, 19

Houlding, John, 10
Hunt, Roger, 13

Keegan, Kevin, 14
Klopp, Jürgen, 22

Mané, Sadio, 24, 26

Origi, Divock, 6, 8
Owen, Michael, 19

Paisley, Bob, 14

Rush, Ian, 18

Salah, Mohamed, 9, 24, 26, 28
Shankly, Bill, 10, 12–14
Shaqiri, Xherdan, 6
Smith, Tommy, 14
Stones, John, 26

van Dijk, Virgil, 24

Wijnaldum, Georginio, 6